Last of the Dinosaurs

The End of an Age

Written by David Eldridge
Illustrated by Norman Nodel

Troll Associates

Pronunciation Guide

Ankylosaurus	(An-kill-uh-SAWR-us)
Brachiosaurus	(Brak-ee-uh-SAWR-us)
Brontosaurus	(Bron-tuh-SAWR-us)
Corythosaurus	(Kor-ith-uh-SAWR-us)
Diplodocus	(Dih-PLAH-duh-kuss)
Stegosaurus	(Steg-uh-SAWR-us)
Trachodon	(TRAK-uh-don)
Triceratops	(Try-SER-uh-tops)
Tylosaurus	(Tie-luh-SAWR-us)
Tyrannosaurus Rex	(Tie-ran-uh-SAWR-us Rex)

Printed in the United States of America. Troll Associates, Mahwah, N.J.
Library of Congress Catalog Card Number: 79-64636
ISBN 0-89375-243-6   (0-89375-247-9 soft cover ed.)

Millions of years ago—long before there were any people on the earth — the world was full of dinosaurs. These huge reptiles ruled the earth for a very long time. About 160 million years went by, from the first dinosaur that lived to the last one. This long period of time is called the Age of Dinosaurs.

Not all the creatures that lived in the Age of Dinosaurs were dinosaurs. Some were queer-looking reptiles that swam in the water. Others were strange flying reptiles that soared through the skies on leathery wings. But there were hundreds of different kinds of dinosaurs on the land. As some kinds died out, others took their place.

Dinosaurs came in all shapes and sizes. Some were almost as long as a city block. Others were the size of chickens or dogs. Some walked on two legs. Others walked on all fours. Some ate only plants—like ferns, mosses, soft bark, and palm-like leaves. Others ate only meat—usually the flesh of other dinosaurs.

The huge plant-eating dinosaurs made the earth thunder as they lumbered through lush swamps and marshy forests. Brachiosaurus was the heaviest of all. It weighed about 85 tons. Diplodocus was the longest animal ever to walk the earth. It was 90 feet long — about ten times as long as an elephant.

But the king of all the dinosaurs was Tyrannosaurus
Rex. Its head was as long as
a man's body. With 6-
inch-long teeth, it could tear
huge chunks of meat from its
prey. Most of the giant
plant-eaters headed for safety when Tyrannosaurus ar-
rived. But some, like Triceratops, might stand and
fight. This three-horned dinosaur had bony armor to
protect itself from the savage
meat-eaters.

For well over 100 million years, the dinosaurs ruled the earth.
But then a mysterious thing began to happen. More and more
dinosaurs began to die. Scientists say that within a few million
years, all the dinosaurs were dead. The sea reptiles and the
flying reptiles died out, too. They became extinct — they no
longer existed.

Why did the Age of Dinosaurs come to an end? Why did dinosaurs in every part of the world become extinct? The earth's surface was changing. But the changes took place gradually — over many millions of years. Other forms of life adjusted and survived. Why didn't the mighty dinosaurs? Scientists have several possible reasons for what has been called "the time of the great dying."

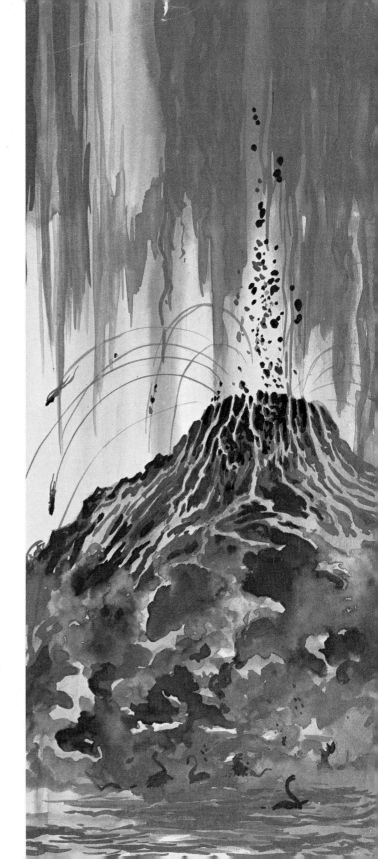

The climate during the Age of Dinosaurs was warmer than it is today. In North America, much of the land was covered by a great shallow sea. Thousands of dinosaurs lived near the warm waters of this sea, in the swamps along its marshy shores. In other parts of the world, dinosaurs lived in other steaming swamps and prehistoric marshes.

Then, ever so slowly, the world changed. It took millions of years, but great forces inside the earth made continents, like North America, rise. The shallow inland American sea began to drain away. To the west, the earth heaved, folded, and pushed up — and the Rocky Mountains were born. All over the world, continents rose, and warm inland seas drained away.

At first, these changes did not bother the dinosaurs. But as the centuries passed, new generations of dinosaurs began to find life harder. The warm, swampy lowlands—with their plentiful food—were disappearing. More and more reptiles found themselves on land that was higher and drier than they were used to.

The world was also getting colder. The cooler temperatures helped kill off many dinosaurs. Unable to move as quickly in the colder climate, big plant-eaters like Corythosaurus grew sluggish. They could not find the energy to fill their great bodies with food. Many fell easy prey to the mighty jaws of Tyrannosaurus.

As the land heaved up and the temperatures cooled down, new kinds of plants and trees developed. In earlier days, there had been palm-like shrubs and trees that were green all year long. Now, hardwood trees, like elms and maples, took their place. For nearly half the year, these new trees had no leaves for the dinosaurs to eat.

The plant-eating dinosaurs could not change their diets quickly enough. They could not get used to the new plants. So they began dying out in great numbers. When they died, there was less food for the meat-eaters. When the plant-eaters were finally extinct, Tyrannosaurus and other meat-eaters must have turned on each other. And soon, they also became extinct.

Life in the water also changed. As the inland seas drained away, smaller lakes were left in the hollow parts of the continents. All over the world, warm tropical waters grew colder. Great sea reptiles, like the 30-foot Tylosaurus, could not move as quickly in cold water. The fish they once caught easily were now too fast for them. So the sea reptiles died out.

In one way or another, the great reptiles of the land, sea, and air, all died. But why did they all die out at about the same time? Scientists can only guess at the answers. Perhaps a sudden, deadly disease killed the reptiles, without affecting other animals, like birds and fish.

But not all the pieces of the puzzle fit. Some reptiles *did* survive "the time of the great dying." These were the ancestors of today's crocodiles, lizards, snakes, and turtles. Of all the reptiles that lived in the Age of Dinosaurs, only these smaller species, or kinds, survived. Why did all the great dinosaurs die? No one knows for sure.

Perhaps their huge size was the reason. During the Age of
Dinosaurs, many dinosaurs grew to enormous sizes. Bronto-
saurus grew bigger and heavier. So did Tyrannosaurus and
Triceratops. They needed more and more food — and food was
becoming harder and harder to find. Many dinosaurs probably
could not keep their huge appetites satisfied.

Although many dinosaurs grew bigger, they did not grow any smarter. Their brains were tiny, compared with their bodies. One of the least intelligent was an armored dinosaur — Stegosaurus. Its brain was only about the size of a walnut. Many experts believe the dinosaurs became extinct because they were not smart enough to change their habits.

The dinosaurs had become set in their ways. When it came time for them to adjust to new conditions, they could not do so. With their large bodies and small brains, the dinosaurs could not get used to the changing times. They could not survive in a world that was changing more rapidly than they were.

It was easier for small animals with large brains to adapt to the changing world. These were the mammals. The mammals were warm-blooded, active, and clever. For centuries, they had lived by their wits, keeping out of the way of the huge dinosaurs.

The mammals probably even helped kill off the dinosaurs. Dinosaurs laid their eggs on top of the ground, and left them to hatch. It was easy for the mammals to sneak in and eat the unprotected eggs. Other dinosaurs probably also ate the eggs— especially when food was scarce. And if all the eggs were eaten before they hatched, no new dinosaurs could be born. The huge reptiles would quickly become extinct.

One scientist — an astrono-
mer — has another theory
about why the dinosaurs
became extinct. Suppose a
star exploded, and its rays
ripped away some of the
earth's air. For a time, the
earth would lose some of its
heat. This would cause a
brief, wintry spell all over
the world. The warm-
blooded mammals could survive, but some cold-blooded
dinosaurs could not.

Imagine what it must have been like 65 million years ago. An aging Trachodon — one of the last of the plant-eating dinosaurs — has been searching all day for leaves and soft bark to eat. Cold and tired, it has dragged itself from one maple forest to another. Its scaly, brownish hide hangs loosely on its large bones. The Trachodon needs food. It has not eaten for several days.

The web-footed ancestors of this dinosaur lived in tropical swamps. They scooped up tender water plants with their broad bills. But this Trachodon lives in a maple forest, where there is nothing but tough bark and dry leaves. The Trachodon staggers on. Then — too late — the old plant-eater hears the stomping of heavy feet behind him.

A young Tyrannosaurus has been stalking the old Trachodon.
Now the hungry meat-eater opens its hungry jaws and attacks.
Its dagger-like teeth sink into the side of the Trachodon. The old
dinosaur puts up a weak struggle, and gives its last shudder.
Then the attacker starts tearing off chunks of meat. Finally, its
hunger is satisfied.

The young Tyrannosaurus drinks from a brook after its meal, and then falls asleep. A large, shadowy figure looms above him. It is another Tyrannosaurus. This full-grown adult has also been looking for food. The sleeping dinosaur never has a chance. Sharp teeth rip savagely into its flesh.

The big Tyrannosaurus has been lucky. With most of the big plant-eaters gone, food has been hard to find. At least today, there will be a meal. After the huge meat-eater has pulled off most of the flesh from its victim's bones, it moves on. A moment later, tiny mammals dart out of the underbrush toward the bones.

Tyrannosaurus covers several miles over the next five days. But it can find nothing to eat. On the sixth day, crazed with hunger, it chases an Ankylosaurus into a thick grove of oaks. Normally, Tyrannosaurus would not bother with this small horned dinosaur—but food is food. The great jaws snap shut—but the Ankylosaurus runs to safety.

The angry Tyrannosaurus pushes deeper and deeper into the forest, chasing anything that moves. Slowly starving to death, it thrashes about and crashes through the trees. When the sharp-eyed little mammals find the body of the great reptile, it is wedged between two oak trees. Time has run out.

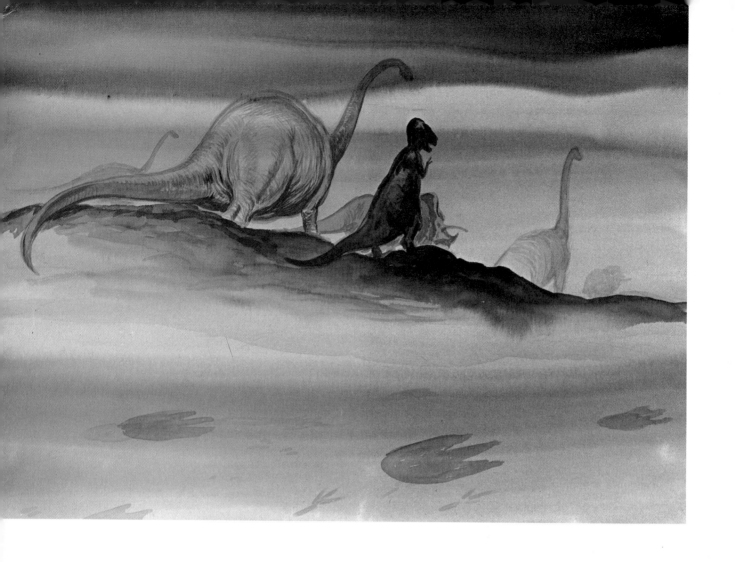

Life became too difficult for even the mightiest of the dinosaurs. One by one, the great reptiles met their end, and finally, they became extinct. Why? Scientists are still not sure exactly how or why it happened. But after 160 million years, the reign of these mighty reptiles was over.